The Mackerel Fishery Of North America, Its Perils And Its Rescue: A Lecture

Shebnah Rich

In the interest of creating a more extensive selection of rare historical book reprints, we have chosen to reproduce this title even though it may possibly have occasional imperfections such as missing and blurred pages, missing text, poor pictures, markings, dark backgrounds and other reproduction issues beyond our control. Because this work is culturally important, we have made it available as a part of our commitment to protecting, preserving and promoting the world's literature. Thank you for your understanding.

THE MACKEREL FISHERY

OF

NORTH AMERICA.

Its Perils and Its Rescue.

A LECTURE,

READ BEFORE THE

MASSACHUSETTS FISH AND GAME ASSOCIATION
OF BOSTON,

BY SHEBNAH RICH.

PRINTED BY REQUEST OF THE ASSOCIATION.

BOSTON:
W. F. BROWN & CO., PRINTERS,
NO. 113 FRANKLIN STREET.

ADDRESS.

LADIES AND GENTLEMEN. — I am aware that my subject has not the popular favor that attracts the multitude, nor can I promise to make you laugh or cry, or steal your sympathies in behalf of my cause. I must speak your forbearance and patience in justice to my subject, at the risk of injustice to myself, while I call your attention to THE MACKEREL FISHERY OF NORTH AMERICA, ITS PERILS AND ITS RESCUE.

Scientists tell us, that to the lowest class in the sub-kingdom of animal life, belong the fishes. We infer that even in this low plane of life, there are orders and castes, just as in the more favored Mammals, embracing man and quadrupeds; and that in the most respectable ranks of fishes, the mackerel and cod are representative members. This claim might be still further predicated on the accepted principle, that to the highest ranks belong those, who confer the highest good. We incline to go a step further, and claim also honorable distinction for the fish, over the quadruped, in a generic sense, on account of ancient ancestry. Ancestry has a pronounced value in this world, in men and horses; why not in fishes.

With patient toil, Irving traces the family of George Washington to the early days of the Plantagenet Kings. Gibbon, with still greater pains-taking, traces the robber factions of the Guelphes, and Ghibelines, nearly a thousand years, to the British throne; making the present Royal family of England, the oldest in Europe. The path, it is true, leads through fire and smoke, and like the old Roman roads, over the mountains, and through the swamp; but it leads straight.

"Pocahontas," who was sold a few years since to Mr. Bonner, for thirty-three thousand dollars, and which I presume still stands in his stables, has probably the best horse pedigree in the world. The late sale of a short-horn Dutchess, of Hillhurst, for twenty-one thousand five hundred dollars, the English papers say, "was solely on account of fashionable pedigree."

Agassiz's patient plough-share turns up families rich in amorial bearings, perhaps a million of years ere Adam began his nomenclature, or the Arabian Emir wrote, "Behold he draweth up a river and boasteth not; he trusteth he can draw up Jordan into his mouth."

Some of these, are such old Saurian families, as the Schindorians and Ichthosarians with eyes forty inches in circumference, leaders of society in their days, who effected distinction by swimming with paddles, instead of fins, like other fish. Near neighbors were the Megolasarians, forty, or five hundred feet long, not particular as to length; the Ptuodectyls, were also of that plastic period.

We are not able exactly to trace the line of relationship between the mackerel and these entombed fossils, but have no doubt it is all direct and simple enough by evolution. Seriously, we hope not to be understood as attempting to prove any of these points, or that the fish, measured by to-day's standard, outranks the horse, or man. We simply state his claims, and submit them to consideration.

Standards at best, are but fashions of slower growth. Some Capt. Boyton of your family tree, may stride a domesticated dolphin on the Charles, with the same pride and grace you curb your favorite Pegasus sweeping down the Brighton Road.

The transition is extraordinary, I grant, but not much more so, than Harvard or Columbia's undergraduate of fifty years ago, in silk cap and hose, and Harvard's bow-oar of to-day, stripped like a galley slave, with the brawn and muscle of a gladiator.

Round-head Prynne (Prynne's *Annum Regime*) records, "in the taking of a whale on the coasts, which is a royal fish, it shall be divided between the King and Queen, the head only being the King's property, and the tail, the Queen's."

The reason of this division was to furnish the Queen's wardrobe with whalebone. So perish the standards of fashion in king's households.

We propose, this evening, to discuss to some extent, the history of the mackerel, their commercial value, the present perils that beset the business, and how to meet them.

Though an animal of the lower order, and little known to fame, we have no doubt a fair investigation will award them a respectable niche in science and history, and no insignificant place physically, educationally, and politically. We shall, however, consider, more particularly, their industrial and commercial relations.

In the American Academy of Art and Science, Vol. 5, Part 1st, we find a history of the fishes of Massachusetts, by David Humphrey Storer, M. D., A. A. S., from which we quote a scientific description of the species of mackerel,—*Scomber vernales*.

"Color,—upper part of the body of a dark green color, marked throughout its whole extent, from the occiput to the tail, with beautiful transverses, more or less undulating, broken bands of a deeper hue, commencing on the side of the dorsal ridge, and extending downward below the lateral lines. Top of head of a dark, almost black color, produced by longitudinal, broad, broken bands, passing backwards from the snout, and a large black blotch extending backwards from the occiput towards the gill-covers. The portion of the head directly back of the eyes, cupreous, gill-covers and maxillery bones, silvery. Intermaxillery bones dark, fuliginous, as well as the tongue and inside of the jaws; angle of the jaws, dusky, sides white, with cupreous reflection, abdomen, white. Beneath the lateral line, on each side in a fuliginous, oftentimes interrupted line, much wider than the lateral line, arising beneath the pictoral fin, and transversing the length of the fish; the space between these two lines is of a duller color than the side beneath.

"This beautiful species is one of the most valuable fishes which frequent our waters."

The historic mackerel made his best flip in America with his insatious friend, the conservative codfish, to the great delight of the Pilgrims and Puritans, in their exceeding time of need; a kind service their sons and daughters are not soon inclined to forget. Consequently the mackerel needs no introduction to a Boston audience. Physically, they are not unworthy your attention or criticism, independent of a scientific description.

Look at the mackerel as it drops from the fisherman's hook. See how it quivers with fear, and struggles in its new element for liberty. Mark the harmony and perfection of every line. A perfect model, according to the most approved rules of modern naval architecture. Sharp ends fore and aft, good floor, not much dead rise, a clean run, carries no dead water, steers easy, fine sea-boat, and sails like a fish.

Behold nature's rich endowment and profusion of painting. Satin-silver to the lateral lines, then flashing to sapphire, emerald, and cerulean. But the mackerel was made for food, as well as beauty, and fast sailing. Perhaps you have never eaten a mackerel. Not the limpy, pale-eyed fish, maticulated at Commercial Wharf or Fulton Market, and graduated up-town after a course on ice, and sold for mackerel.

I mean a plump, muscular, number one, of the old-fashioned cull; caught in the sun-rise spurt, dressed and corned ship-shape, and fisherman-fashion; curled up on the taffrail, just right for supper, and in full flavor. That's food fit for Jupiter. "There's eating for you," as the Indian said to the Frenchman whose brother he had eaten for breakfast.

Of all the finny tribes that roam or sport in the ocean, the mackerel is the most beautiful, eatable, and valuable. While fresh, it is found upon the table of the rich and poor, many months in the year; affording always a healthy and desirable, sometimes a delicious, and often for months, an exceedingly cheap kind of food. Fresh mackerel have been sold in London Market, as high as seven shillings each, and as low as sixty for one shilling.

In 1833, sixteen boats carried into the London Market, mackerel valued at twenty-five thousand dollars, caught in a single day. In 1864, a boat carried in one night, mackerel that sold for over five hundred dollars.

Unlike most other fish, mackerel, when salted, are merchantable in any climate of the world, and consequently become a world-wide article of commerce. Though only an annual visitor, yet like other fashionable visitors, they come North to spend the season, and linger till chill waters give warning of coming snow and ice. Where they spend their winters, is a conundrum. Perhaps this association will offer a silver speaking-trumpet to the lucky discoverer. Sure it is, none have been interviewed, or have communicated after leaving our shores fat and plump, till they return with the spring birds, starving poor, like the Prodigal Son.

Prof. Mitchell, and Dr. Dickey describe the spring and autumn mackerel of Massachusetts shore, as distinct species. With this opinion, Prof. Storer first agrees, then hesitates, and finally decides that they are the same species; thus, sensibly concurring in the unanimous and unquestioned opinion of fishermen, on this point.

"The Aboriginal name of mackerel was wawwunuekeseag, signifying 'fatness,' but that species of fat peculiar to the belly, a very descriptive and appropriate name, its continued roundness even to the tail, being a striking feature."

Isaac Allerton, of the Mayflower band, is the first to mention mackerel in the Western world. He sat up a station at Hull, in 1626, (better now known "as goes Hull, so goes the State,") where he seined mackerel by moon-light. Seining or netting fish seems the oldest method on record. It was the favorite mode of the disciples as recorded in the New Testament. And Christ has taught some of his most forcible lessons by referring to this oriental custom. It was almost, if not entirely, the only way of catching mackerel for the first hundred years or more, after the settlement of the Colonies.

The ship Arabella, of historic fame, left the Downes, Easter Monday, March 29th, 1629. With this date John Winthrop commences his Journal to America.

June 11, he writes, "The Isles of Shoales are now within two leagues of us. We took many mackerels, and met a shollop, which stood from Cape Ann, toward the Isles of Shoales, that belonged to some English fishermen."

"Saturday 12th, Mr. Allerton came on board of us in a shollop, as he was sailing to Pemaquid." Isaac Allerton was the pioneer mackerel fisherman of the New World, and should be the fisherman's patron-saint. Twenty-five years later, a reckord is found, for a receipt from him, for one hogshead and four barrels of mackerel. Pemaquid, referred to by Mr. Winthrop, in connection with Menhegan, were two famous fishing stations on the coast of Maine, where the English had fished for cod many years.

In 1623, Sir Ferdinando Gorges, whose name is so often found in connection with the first settlements of New England, had a plantation on the Island of Menhegan, which had long been a noted resort for ships fishing on the Coast. Gorges was the original proprietor to a grant in his own undivided right, to territory between the Piscataqua and Kennebec, which he called "Maine," in honor of Queen Henrietta's estate in France. He was a member of the Plymouth Council, and has sometimes been represented as a grasping and unscrupulous member of that Company. It is only justice to a noble representative Englishman, the boldest and most enterprising of his age, to say, nothing could be farther from the truth.

Sir Ferdinando was not a Puritan, but a stanch Episcopal, and a firm believer in the Stuarts, whom, I need not say, every Puritan hated with the intense bitterness of their age. It is doubtless owing to this fact, that his reputation has sometimes suffered in history.

The Gilberts and the Pophams, Challon, Vine, and Dermer, all men of great enterprise, and brave navigators, who established fisheries at Menhegan, on our Coast, before the Mayflower sailed for America, were of this same political and religious stripe.

In 1626, Robert Aldworth and Giles Elbridge, two eminent merchants of Bristol, Eng., purchased in the interests of the fisheries, the Island of Menhegan. They soon after obtained a patent of lands at Pemaquid, known as the "Pemaquid Patent," being seven thousand acres of land, on the maine, and all the islands within nine leagues of the shore. A flourishing Colony was established at Pemaquid. Their descendants are still in possession of the allotments made to their ancestors under the patent.

These references show that the fisheries were among the early inducements to colonize New England.

Capt. John Smith established a station at Pemaquid, in 1614, six years before the settlement of Plymouth. Smith intended to catch whale, in which he failed, as the season was well advanced. But Capt. John Smith was a man of resources, and if he could not catch whale, would catch the next best thing, which in this case was codfish; so he set his men to fishing.

They caught and cured twelve hundred quintals, that sold in Spain for five dollars per quintal. While his men were catching fish, Smith, in a small boat, coasted along the shores from Penobscot to Cape Cod. For trifles of little value, he traded with the natives, securing eleven thousand bear skins, eleven hundred martins, and many other valuable commodities; besides gaining important knowledge of the coast, which resulted in his valuable map of New England

In command of a Polaristic expedition, Capt. John Smith would push his way to the North Pole, take accurate measurements thereof, gauge the Polar Sea, and return to pay a dividend on the outfit. Could Mr. Bennett secure such a leader, Stanley with all his honest claim to world-wide favor would stand eclipsed. Instead of a broken-hearted old man peddling a history of his own strangely marvellous life about England, urging the colonization of the Western world, we should see Guild and Exeter Hall waiting to open their doors, and the Lord Mayor of London welcoming so worthy a son to the freedom of the Mansion House.

The Rev. Francis Higginson, first minister of Salem, who came in the ship "Tolbot," in 1629, author of the famous saying, "A sup of New England's aire is better than a whole draft of Old England's ale," says in his "New England Plantation," "such an abundance of mackerels that it would astonish one to behold."

In 1633, the ship "William" set up a station at Scituate, where mackerel were taken freely with the seine. Dr. Douglass, who wrote in about 1750, of New England, refers at considerable length, to the mackerel, which he calls a "capricious and sportive fish." He says, "being at Plymouth, June 27th, we made the following notes of the dimensions and weight of fresh mackerel, of three several sizes in the market, as follows:

First size, length in inches, 18; circuit " " 10; weight 2 lb. 10 oz.

Second size, length in inches, 16; circuit " " 8; weight 1 lb. 8 oz.

Third size, length in inches, 14; circuit " " 7; weight 1 lb.

We wish old Isaac Allerton and John Winthrop had left on record, as accurately, the size of the old Colonial fish.

In 1836, Hon. Caleb Cushing, our late octogenarian minister to Spain, was representative in Congress. He presented a "Bill in addition to an act to authorize the licensing of vessels to be employed in the mackerel fishery."

The object of this Bill was to secure to all vessels engaged in the mackerel fishery, the same privilege of Government Bounty, as were allowed to vessels engaged in the cod fishery.

This was simple justice and equity, as it was plainly and entirely, the intention of the law to pay a bounty on the consumption of salt, and encourage a valued home industry. More important still was it to the young nation, to cultivate, in time of peace, a hardy class of seamen, ready for an ocean police, in the hour of danger.

Mr. Cushing ably defended the bill, showing that the mackerel fishery had been developed since the passage of the Bounty act, and that all the reasons that applied to a Bounty upon codfish, applied with equal force to mackerel.

Through jealousy, or hostility, the bill was lost, and a few years later, without the shadow of a reason, Congress repealed the Government Bounty altogether, In his remarks, Mr. Cushing expatiated freely upon the mackerel fishers, and said, "The movements and haunts of the mackerel are more precarious, and their habits more versatile than those of any other fish of commercial importance. So true is this, that fishermen who have pursued the business for a long period, have but little advantage over those who have recently engaged in it, in judging with any degree of certainty, which may be the best spot of fishing ground at any season of the year."

We can find no fault with the first part of this statement. To the last part, possibly the fisherman would say, that fortunately for Mr. Cushing, his reputation does not depend upon what he knows about mackerel.

It used to be said of Amsterdam, that it was built upon herring bones, and that Dutchmen were made of pickled herrings. The rich old Dutch Burghers esteemed it a fine compliment, as their vast wealth had been acquired through the herring fishery.

It was the success of these fisheries more than any other cause, that excited the enterprise of England in the sixteenth century, and led to her Golden Age of discoveries. History tells us of fishermen laying the foundations of many ancient cities, generations before the Northern Vikings were born.

"Not a century had elapsed since the fishermen emerged from their bogs, and they had acquired greater dominion than Rome won by their arms in the long course of two hundred years."—*Gibbon on the Genoese.*

In 1860, the exports of Liverpool, from her own manufactures, was three hundred millions of dollars. Twenty-five thousand sail of shipping entered her docks, that range seven miles of tide-water, covering four hundred and twenty acres, and costing one hundred millions of dollars. Our English cousins set a good example in bold enterprise, whether public or private. The dashing purchase of the Suez Canal is an instance of the former.

Sympathize as we may, let the result be what it may, credit whom we will: with England holding the key to Ormus and Ind; the land of the Ptolemys and Pyramids; the Bear with her strong paw on the Golden Horn and Bosphorus as hostages, and Prussia as the balance of power in Europe as a guarantee for fair play, there is hope for the peace of the world and the spread of Christianity and civilization. Thank God, that a Christian nation, ruling two hundred millions of the human race, in spite of other faults, has come to see something of true national grandeur.

Liverpool is newer than our Atlantic cities. Less than two hundred years ago, fishermen built their huts, hauled up their boats, and spreads their nets, where now stands that gate-way of commerce, and where enter the rich-freighted argosies of the world. Roscoe with his genius and wealth, did much for Liverpool, but the English fishermen founded it.

The mackerel was early an active agent in the Education of New England. In 1660, Commissioners of the Colony of New England recommended to the General Court of the Confederacy to regulate this branch of the fishery in the following

Chapter. "An abstract of the laws of New England, as they are now established. Printed in London, 1641. Chapter III., of the Protection and Provision of the Country. Because fishing is the chief staple commodity of the Country, therefore all due encouragement to be given unto such hands as shall set forward the trade of fishing : and for the end a law to be made, that whomsoever shall apply themselves to set forward the trade of fishing, as fishermen, mariners and shipwrights, shall be allowed man for man, or some other of the laborers of the country to plant and reap for them in the season of the year at the public charge of the Commonwealth, for the space of the seven years next ensuing; and such laborers to be appointed and paid by the Treasurer of the Commonwealth."

The "Trial," the first ship built in Boston in 1633, made a yoyage to Bilboa and Malaga, laden with fish, and returned with a cargo of wine, fruit, oil, iron, and wool, which was a great advantage to the new Colonies, and great encouragement to their struggling commerce. "In 1652, a law provided for the appointment of sworn Fish-Viewers, at every fishing place within the jurisdiction, who were required to reject all unmerchantable, all sun-burnt, salt-burnt and dry fish that hath been first pickled, to be paid one half by the dealer, the other half by the receiver."

For many years preceding 1775, the trade, from codfish alone, furnished the Northern Colonists with nearly half their remittances for British manufactures, and was the life-blood of commerce.

About this time, the mackerel fishing at Cape Cod was held by the Colony of Plymouth as public property, and rented to the fishermen, and its profits appropriated to public purposes. For more than a hundred years after the settlement of Plymouth, that section of the Cape now embracing Provincetown, was known as Cape Cod. Within fifty years the elderly people of Truro, and the neighboring towns, used to speak of Provincetown as "the Cape." The privileges of fishing were duly regulated and the renting was made from time to time for agreed sums.

The first free school established by our Pilgrim Fathers, was supported from these proceeds. This proposition was first made in 1663. In 1670, the General Court, "Upon due and serious consideration, did freely give and grant all such profits as might or shall annually accrue to the Colony, from time to time, for fishing with nets or seines at Cape Cod for mackerel, bass or herrings, to be improved, for and towards a FREE SCHOOL in some town of this jurisdiction, for the training of the youth in literature, for the good and benefit of posterity, provided a beginning be made within one year after said grant." In June, 1674, this grant was confirmed by the following record: "This Court having received by the duputies of the several towns, the signification of the minds of the major part of the freemen of the Colony, that all the profits of the fishing at Cape Cod, granted by the Court, for the erecting and maintaining a school, do hereby confirm the grant of the aforesaid profits of the fishing at the Cape, to the maintainance of the school, and that there be no further demands, besides the said profits of the Cape on the County, for the maintainance of the said school." "In 1678, five pounds, silver money of the Cape fishing rent was paid to Mrs. Newman, widow of Rev. Noah Newman, of Rehoboth, and five pounds to Rehoboth schoolmaster. "In 1680, ten pounds silver money was received from Cornet Robert Stetson, and Nathaniel Thomas, rent of Cape fishing, a part of which went to pay for a piece of land at the Cape for the Colony, and the residue to the school." "In 1682, the rent of Cape fishing was added to the appropriations for the magistrate's salary for that year."

Here was built the foundation of that system of education, that has become a common inheritance.

> "Himself from God he could not free;
> He builded better than he knew;
> The conscious stone to beauty grew."

If the Pilgrims did not build better than they knew, it must be admitted that they knew better how to build than any before them. Without claiming them faultless, or possessed of all wisdom, they need no apology. They stand safely on their merits. We think of no great principle in civil or religious liberty, that was not wafted in the Mayflower, and planted on Plymouth Rock.

The founding of Free Schools was in harmony with the wisdom of the Forefathers. They knew that general education was a great force in religious and political enlightenment, and in the elevation of the race. True to these convictions, they made possible a noble standard, thereby to bless the brotherhood of man, and glorify the fatherhood of God. They had faith in God. "Faith in God is the true architect of greatness for men and nations; for this world, as well as the world to come. This is the Star in the East that brings to a Saviour; that amid difficulties and dangers, and bewilderments and storms, shines true forever, over the pilgrimages of individuals and empires. Duty, and duty alone, is great, safe and mighty. Man is strong as he holds God's hands,—lofty as he bows before Him,—wise as he listens only to His voice,—true liberty is His science,—true order His law,—true life His love."

In 1689, the rent of the Cape fisheries were again added to the appropriations for the Magistrate's salary for that year. But for this husbanding of resources, and patching with Yankee frugality, the young Colony might have been embarrassed by a government loan. As our first Free Schools were founded and nursed upon mackerel, Boston was founded and nursed upon codfish. Our early Statesmen accepted this fact with pride, and lest their children should forget it, suspended the codfish, still fronting the Speaker's Chair in the House. As a companion piece, a mackerel fronting the other Chair, would be in harmony, and would be tardy justice, like the monuments to Miles Standish, Roger Williams, and other great contemporaries. The codfish referred to was first placed in the Old State House, on motion of John Rowe, Esq., then a member of the House, a merchant of Boston, who for many years supplied the fishermen with salt, hooks and lines.

William of Orange, offered the City of Leyden, in common with the low Countries, who had fought through the bloodiest and perhaps the noblest struggle for liberty on record, immunities from taxes, that she might recover from the drain of war. Leyden declined the offer, and asked for the privilege of erecting a University within her walls, as the best reward for more than human endurance. This has been placed in history, to the imperishable honor of Leyden.

What shall be the reward of those few men on the shores of a new Continent, amid perils of poverty, war and oppression, meditating and inaugurating a system of free education, which has distinguished their posterity the world over, and planted schools and universities till the wilderness and the solitary places have budded and blossomed as the rose?

About 1784, a series of anonymous Essays on Commerce appeared in one of the Boston papers, since understood to have been written by James Swan, Esq., a member of the General Court, from Dorchester. One of these Essays was devoted to the fisheries, in which he says: "The mackerel is of more value to Massachusetts than would be the pearl fishery of Ceylon." Some of the other papers noticed the remark "as a felicity of expression," thinking, no doubt, they had suppressed Mr. Swan. Let us see what has been the direct and indirect result of this "felicity of expression." In 1851, there were engaged in the Massachusetts mackerel fishery, eight hundred and fifty-three vessels of fifty-three thousand seven hundred tons, employing about ten thousand men. Probably none of that fleet are now in the business. Like men, they drop one by one, out of their accustomed places, scarcely missed at the time, but in a few years, all are gone. They have been replaced by a much larger and better class of nautical craft.

To fully appreciate the present fleet engaged in mackerel catching, they should be seen beating into the harbor with a spanking breeze, or working up to windward, on the ground, so as to keep on the school, which seems always going to the windward, while the fleet constantly drop to the leeward. Their long, sharp, graceful hulls, taunt, jaunty spars, flat, trim sails, and lively manœuvring would suggest an ocean regatta of clever yachts.

We are without complete statistics, but making up by carefully prepared estimates, there were in the Massachusetts mackerel fishery, in 1874, not less than one thousand vessels of nearly one hundred thousand tons, o. m., employing fifteen thousand men. The cost of this fleet, with seines, boats, and entire outfit, would not fall short of ten millions of dollars. In addition, we have the shore preparations of boats, nets, seines, weirs, etc. ; besides a large number of vessels belonging to Maine, and other New England States, swelling the cost to probably thirteen millions.

There has been inspected in Massachusetts alone, during the ten years preceeding, and including 1874, two millions three hundred and sixteen thousand and eighty-three barrels, an average of two hundred and thirty-one thousand, six hundred barrels annually. At an average price of twelve dollars and a half per barrel, which must be conceded a low estimate for these years, we have an annual product of about three millions from the salt mackerel department of Massachusetts. In 1850, Prof. Storer estimated, that about eight thousand barrels of fresh mackerel were sold in the Boston market.

Since 1850, owing to increased facilities for transportation, and the general use of ice, this branch has been augmented in Boston at least ten-fold. Immense quantities are carried direct to the New York market during the spring and early summer, counting which, and other places, it would seem a safe calculation, that at least half as many mackerel are now sold fresh, as are salt-packed. Estimating their value the same as the salted fish, and allowing only half a million for all the mackerel caught in Maine and the other States, we have five millions of dollars annual income, to the industry of the State, on an outlay of thirteen millions. This five million is purely productive; every dollar comes from the ocean. Not even farming is so pre-eminently and entirely a productive industry. The fisherman ploughs an untaxed furrow that needs no replenishing year by year.

It is said the pearl fishers get the smallest share of the valuable pearls. So it may be said of our fishermen, they get the smallest share of the money, and are probably the poorest paid, on an average, of any class of men in the country. This does not affect the value of the industry to the State or country at large, but rather proves its distributing tendency, and indirect interests. Among the indirect interests, we have the building and equipping, annually, of hundreds of vessels, costing probably from three to ten thousand dollars, and thousands of boats, dories, etc.

The forging of anchors and chains, the spinning of huge cables, cordage, and lines, the weaving of millions of yards of seines and nets, that employ thousands of women and children, the running of mills to manufacture duck to be fitted by the handy skill of the sail-maker, the fleet of ocean vessels employed by importers of salt; the towns in Massachusetts and New Hampshire engaged in the manufacture of cooperage, that have become enriched thereby; the handling annually by packets and railroads of fifty to sixty thousand tons of freight, the consumption of fifty thousand tons of ice, and a host of outfitters, packers, and laborers at all the fishing outposts, making up in part a list of industries which need a constantly cherishing hand.

Of the capital and men employed in all these indirect and diversified interests, we have attempted no calculation; nor have we referred to the direct trade which has its merchants in every city in the land, from Portland, Maine, to its sister namesake on the Pacific coast. The aggregate capital involved must be surely half a hundred million of dollars. The one universal method or custom, followed during the highest development of mackerel catching, was with the simple hook and line from the vessel; now called "hooking," in distinction from "seining," that has so completely outrivaled the old way.

Catching mackerel is dexterous work, and to become an expert, requires nimble movements. All the individual arms, hands and fingers are needed in full play.

Lord Nelson, who had lost an arm, was once visiting a hospital, and finding one of his sailors short an arm, by a cannon ball, he said, "Jack, you and I are spoiled for fishermen."

It is almost incredible how fast mackerel may be caught by a trained crew. The mackerel sometimes go up so fast, that the whole side of the vessel shines like silver. In July, 1842, a crew of eleven men and boys "struck a school" of biting mackerel on Gorges Bank. In twenty-five minutes they caught thirty strike-barrels (a barrel so full that the live mackerel jump out.) One of the boys referred to, is well known to the writer, and is good authority.

Ten hours such fishing would give six hundred strike-barrels or about three hundred barrels, which at the present price of that quality, would stock seven thousand five hundred dollars. Among leading mackerel fishermen, Skipper Richard Rich, of Truro, was a celebrity in his day. For many years he was "high line" in the country. On account of sailing many years in the schooner Osceola, he became quite widely known as "Osceola Dick"; some thought that mackerel knew him as well, and came to his hook.

One hundred and fifty wash-barrels was not a great deck for Osceola Dick. He has taken one hundred and ninety wash-barrels in a single day, all saved in good order, and without feeling very fishy. I would not contract to make one of those old "lucky skippers" believe Mr. Cushing's doctrine, that one man knew just as well as another where to find mackerel. They knew better. In the old hooking days, there used to be skippers that always found fish, and never missed a comfortable income, however hard the season. Possibly — probably, they were not all scholars or statesmen — perhaps not all saints, but they knew where to find fish, and how to catch them.

The art in fishing may be learned, but uniform success is genius, and must be inborn, or in technical phraseology, a lucky skipper must be "fishy." It was estimated that seventy thousand barrels of mackerel were caught on the hook in one week, several years ago, on Jeffrey's Ledge, off Cape Cod. These references are sufficient for our purpose, to show that mackerel enough can be secured in the old way, to supply all the markets of the world with millions of barrels, if they will *bite*.

The ready expansion of the fishing business under favorable circumstances, can be well illustrated by the extraordinary growth of the flourishing city of Gloucester, on our northern shore, which has been built up almost entirely within the last fifty years, from the ocean.

In 1830, Gloucester had an inconsiderable tonnage engaged

in the foreign trade, a few coastwise, and about thirty sail of fishing vessels. Now over five hundred sail of able seagoing schooners, the best equipped vessels on the ocean, besides numerous boats and other small craft, make up the most imposing fleet found at any one port in the world. They are found in all American waters, at all seasons of the year, and have even crossed the ocean in search of business. A greater calamity can scarcely be conceived, than a blow to this enterprising community, and its brave, hardy sons.

This brings us to consider carefully the merits of seining, which we have already stated, has outrivaled the hook. Deep sea, or purse seining, was first introduced, perhaps thirty years since. It grew slowly into favor, and was often condemned as impracticable, and a failure. Experience suggested many improvements; and practice, as is always the case, overcome many discouragements. It required, however, much experience, and long practice, to become skilled adepts in the art. It has now become almost a science; and the facility with which a boat will approach a school of fish, and the headsman "throw his twine" of one hundred and eighty-five fathoms by twenty-eight, or ninety-three thousand feet, (about two acres of netting), around and "purse up" is almost marvellous. Many long, weary days, however, does the anxious skipper and his ready crew, watch for schools, without a ripple, and many a time does he "shoot," without pursing a tail. Sometimes, when the fish seem almost secure in the seine, and hearts beat high with hope of a rich haul, like a lightning-flash all are gone. Sometimes an unmannerly shark, like Satan among the sons of men, is there also, and makes a clean dash and breach, letting all free. Sometimes they save part, and occasionally gobble up the entire school. One thousand barrels have been taken at a haul. A Wellfleet fisherman said, they saved three hundred and fifty wash-barrels in good order, out of one school, and were all ready for more the next day at 12 o'clock. The next year, they saved three hundred and twenty-five at one haul. A fisherman related the following incidents of his experience in 1875-6:

"One day, wide of Thatcher's Island, 'bout a wholesale

breeze here sou'west, we shot around a good school of fish. Pursed up lively, and found we had her full thundering great mackerel, and a big sword fish. Old feller began to wind himself up in the twine, and let every fish out that seine in spite of us. You better 'blieve we had a scrape unwinding that old sword fish, and that he got more curses than coppers. We reckoned he spoilt about three thousand dollars for us. 'N other time, found we had a black fish, about twenty-five feet long; it looked like fun, I tell ye; and we counted seine and fish both gone up. He made a rush, and went out like a shot ghost. We pulled up the lint and sure as you live, saved ninety wash-barrels, first-rate fish out that school after all."

That the mackerel is a capricious fish, is just as true now as in 1750 or in 1836. About forty years ago, a custom of "gaffing" was quite generally practiced. As soon as the school was done biting, the experts took their long slim gaffs, and with wonderful precision, and almost lightning dexterity, snatched their victims. It was regarded a barbarous practice; many intelligent and successful skippers would not have a mackerel gaff on board their vessels. They said, with seeming wisdom, that it scared the fish, and was prejudicial to the business. We refer to this experience particularly, to show how sensitive fishermen have been in the past, and how carefully they managed not to break the haunts or disturb the ordinary habits of this sensitive fish.

It would seem a reasonable conclusion, that so many boats in hot pursuit as soon as a mackerel ripples the surface, and dragging such immense masses through the water with the consequent confusion, must greatly excite and disturb such timid fish. This conclusion is still further favored by the fact, that when the fish first touch our coast, they are comparatively quite readily taken; but as the season advances, they become shy and seem to say, "catch us if you can." In September, 1873, an experienced skipper with a fine reputation for seining, states, "that he threw his seine nine times in one day as handsomely as ever in his life, and every time, thought he had 'em sure." Total catch, thirteen hundred. Not unfrequently the seine is loaded with small mackerel, called by the fishermen "spikes," which in ordinary times will not pay for saving. A fisherman of many years experience with seining, and of good judgment, assured me that in the season of 1876, there were more thrown out of the seines than were saved, and he added, "that is one of the worst things about seining."

The effect of such slaughtered hosts filling the valleys of the ocean, being swept by ocean currents, must damage the living tribes, saying nothing of such immense waste of life among the young fish. The destruction of every barrel of these young mackerel is fully equal to eight or ten barrels of large fish. If then, as many small in bulk were thrown out of the seines as were saved, the slaughter would be equivalent to nearly a million barrels of large mackerel in one season. No great wonder there has been a famine of mackerel this season, though the fishermen have been glad to save even the spikes, and have worked hard to do so. A good many fish are thrown away that become too soft to dress, and it often happens that a great haul will be taken when the vessel is nearly full, and if no neighbors are near, the surplus must be thrown overboard.

All these excesses going on in a fleet of more than a thousand vessels, swells the destruction to a monstrous aggregate in some seasons. Complaints are common, that when large hauls are made, and a good many fish thrown on the market, in a few days almost a panic takes place, to the detriment of both the trade and the fishermen. It is claimed that under the old system the markets were more regular and reliable. This may or may not be the fact. The best of mackerel used to be caught in the cool weather of September and October. The choice old-fashioned "Mess" and "Extra" number one, could most always be depended upon sufficiently to supply the market for the year. Few mackerel are seined after August, as a rule, and of late years the market has been comparatively bare of those standard high grades that used to have such a high reputation. The inquiry is repeated from all sections, "Why can't we have such mackerel now-a-days as we used to have?"

Purse seines require deep water and plenty of room. The season of '75 was only saved from failure as complete as '77, by a heavy body of small mackerel very late in the season; but for several weeks during the summer, abundance of fine fish hugged the eastern shore in shallow water, and among the rocks, safe from their enemies. In previous years, when the fish were among the rocks, the fishermen in boats and dories "skowbanged" with great success, making good trips and a profitable season. I cannot say that the fish in '75 were the *biters*, but the fishermen were not prepared to give them a trial, or to secure them if ready to jump into their boats. The outlay for seine and boats is a heavy draft on the owners or outfitters, and the wear and tear a constant expense. A moderately good vessel ready for a voyage, can be bought at about the same cost of new seines and outfits. I know an old skipper that hung to his jig and flyline through all the seine fever high and low. He has never missed an average income, and one or two seasons was among the " high lines."

I have considered carefully, disinterestedly, and fairly, the principal objections, as I understand them, to seining mackerel. My information has been gained by practical experience, and constant observation during the last ten years of seine growth; and more than thirty years of intimate acquaintance with most every branch of the fishing business. There may be different theories, and different arguments, and different experiences, but substantially there can be but one conclusion, and final judgment must be a unit. The unwelcome, stubborn fact stares us in the face, that a great public industry and national interest is seriously jeopardized, and without immediate and radical change, must soon come to ruin.

Many fishermen think, that next season will be a successful one. Compared with the present, we have no doubt of it, as to quantity, but the fish must grow smaller and poorer while seining continues. We do not measure a substantial industry by one year; only by a series of years, can a positive ratio be determined. It is the ratio of a series of years that sounds the sure alarm, and now calls for help. Just what to do with so much invested capital, with so many thousand active men bred to the business, and with so many contingent interests, may not be hastily determined. A healthy and intelligent discussion of the whole question, is, no doubt, all-important, and cannot help hastening the desired result. It is said the fishermen are most interested, that they are eagle-eyed, and have one eye always open to the windward. That they ought to know. For once the fishermen have lost their reckoning and now seek a new departure. Their property is in their vessels and seines, and they have no other business. They must follow it through good and evil report. When the seine began to be adopted, the old fishermen shrugged up their shoulders, like a Frenchman, and looked wise. Their ominous and prophetic "don't know," like the Delphic oracle, could be interpreted good or bad — now, they are all prophets. The fact that seines paid, and were popular, especially with the young, soon swept down the protest of many experienced men. The fishermen are generally prejudiced in favor of the seine. The great hauls often made, and the possibilities any hour of securing a prize, keeps up the excitement of the business like a lottery, and accounts in some measure, for the popular favor and speculation of the seine. It must be remembered, that the old-fashioned bait-mill and bait-box, jig, and fly-line, are a slow train, compared with the new. It is like machinery against hard labor, steam against muscle.

A smart fishermen said, " I had rather go seining for nothing but the fun, than be sure of an old-fashioned voyage hooking." But he had made large profits seining, and the remark indicates only an expression of popular feeling under successful seasons. No doubt the novelty of the new experience broke up the monotony of the proverbial mackerel trip, and if it put more money in the pockets of the fishermen, they were well satisfied indeed. Upon a close investigation, it will be found, that the laws of instinct that govern fish, are quite as wonderful as those belonging to animals. In what school of Natural Philosophy did codfish study the laws of gravitation? How did they learn that deep water is buoyant, and that when in pursuit of food, or for spawning, they quit one bank for another, or for the shores, they must take on ballast like a ship? There is more in common between the dwellers on the land, and in the water, than we are apt to think.

In pursuit of food, mackerel roam the ocean as the beast roams the forests; but they move North or South by laws as fixed as the rule of the seasons. Thoreau, in his "Cape Cod," tells of a Wellfleet farmer, who kept his schooner anchored in sight of his house, and while his corn and potatoes were growing, and at other odd times, with his boys, he ran down to Virginia, and other points along the coast. Thoreau calls the schooner a market-wagon, which this ocean farmer drove amain. As the farmer calls his flock by scattering corn, and thus leads them to fresh pastures and fields anew, so these sea-farmers call their flocks into the bays and on the banks of the coast, and feed with food convenient for them. In other words, the thousand or fifteen hundred sail of fishermen, that used to fringe our shores, and by a systematic practice, scatter a hundred thousand barrels, annually, of fat, fresh-ground food to the mackerel, called "throwing bait," had educated the fish to visit, feed, and fatten in handy pastures. Not much more surely, are the grazing herds on our western prairies and bottoms, to come to the knife, and swell the commerce of the world, than a fair share of these finny herds were sure to come to the hook. That the fishermen coyed the fish, fatted, and kept them generally around our shores, improved the stock, if you please, seems quite evident from the light of experience, and is now quite generally admitted. The conclusion, then, is irresistable, that the abandoning of the old practice of throwing bait, and the resort to seining, has changed the habits of mackerel on our coast, led them considerably to new fishing-grounds farther off-shore, in pursuit of live bait, and accounts for their half-fed condition the last few years, and especially the present season. If further proof is needed, we refer to the well known fact, that the Bay of Chelaur, or Bay of St. Lawrance mackerel, called by way of distinction from "shore fish," "Bay," and "P. E. I." which for many years have been of inferior quality, have been improving the last year or two, and this season have brought the highest price in our markets.

Forty years ago, mackerel were plenty most of the season in Massachusetts and Cape Cod bays. A large fleet of small vessels, embracing "pinkeys," "giggers," and "beetle-noses" used to fish the season through, without going outside of the bay. The last class very much resembled the farmer's "chebacco-boat" having two masts and no bowsprit or spring-stay. Fishing was never more successful than when the mackerel swarmed in the Bay. Some of these small vessels have landed eight hundred barrels during a season, and I have heard of one instance where a Gloucester gigger landed thirteen hundred barrels in one season. Massachusetts Bay of fifty years ago, the last two or three years, has been transferred to the Bay of St. Lawrence; and the boats and small craft of Prince Edward's Island and vicinity have been throwing bait after the Yankee style. The result is, Yankee fish. A simple case of cause and effect. These same changes have taken place before in the history of the mackerel fishery, and singularly enough, have always taken place when the bulk of our fleet were throwing bait in the "Bay," and neglecting our home fishery.

California is a growing market for our mackerel; if our catch was sufficient, as it ought to be, to supply her with fat fish at a reasonable price, the consumption on the western coast would be enormous. Yet there are a plenty of mackerel on the Pacific shore. In the summer of 1859, Capt. J. L. McDonald, author of "Fisheries around the North West Coast," formerly a fisherman from Truro, Massachusetts, while a passenger from Panama to San Francisco, drailed mackerel. Upon his arrival, he fitted out a vessel, and caught, in a few weeks, two hundred and forty-six barrels on the North East side of Santa Cruz Island.

Capt. McDonald says, "The mackerel are lean and poor, and when salted, are hard and tough. Opposite the old Mission of Santa Barbara, we encountered large bodies at times. They appeared to gravitate to the westward, but we have not been able to trace them to any higher lattitude. The scarcity of fat mackerel along the North-west coast is a fatal drawback to our commercial development." It is pretty well determined that the Pacific ocean does not furnish food for mackerel, and as a result, the hard, tough fish caught by Capt. McDonald. The present population, and the future millions, must depend upon the Atlantic coast for their supply.

The same general law applies to mackerel, as to other goods. When plenty and cheap, the business is most successful in all its branches. All the wheels of trade move with plenty of stock at low prices. For years past, No. 1, salt mackerel have sold for more money than No. 1, salmon, which are regarded a luxury. No. 1 mackerel, are selling to-day in Boston market, from seventeen to twenty-five dollars, as to quality, and a very small stock. Considerably higher prices are looked for. The first condition for a fair competition of any great food product, is an abundant supply. There are hundreds of millions to be fed, and the markets of the world are wide open, and ready to discriminate and appreciate the intrinsic value of any staple food commodity. This is the first law of Political Economy — supply and demand. If the supply of good mackerel was adequate, the price would regulate itself, and the demand would not be wanting. In 1835, the Philadelphia market alone took over one hundred thousand barrels from Massachusetts. The same year, the State of Georgia took thirty-seven thousand barrels. So Philadelphia and Georgia took more mackerel in 1835, than were inspected in Massachusetts in 1878. Let us look at this still further in the light of the inexorable logic of figures and tables.

I have stated that the average catch for the ten years, ending with 1874, was two hundred and thirty-one thousand six hundred barrels, and for the ten years, ending with 1833, the average was two hundred and forty-seven thousand six hundred barrels. About sixteen thousand barrels more annually, than in the last decade.

In 1830, the population of the United States was less than thirteen millions; in 1874, it was over forty millions. The same ratio of consumption as in 1833, would require eight hundred and sixty-seven thousand, — in 1877, say one million of barrels. Our whole catch in the English and American waters of North America this season, is not one fifth of that quantity. And probably less than half the number of barrels inspected in Massachusetts, alone in 1833. It must be remembered that, in 1830, there was not a railroad on the Continent. Although the advantages of transportation have increased at a prodigious rate, yet the sales of mackerel have fallen off over three hundred and fifty per cent, per capita.

Fishermen find the first mackerel about the twentieth of

April, in the neighborhood of Cape Henry, Va. Good trips have been caught off Cape May, as early as the twenty-fifth of April, and good fishing at Sandy Hook by the fifth of May. Nearly all the mackerel caught up to the middle of May, are now carried fresh to New York market. From the twentieth to the last of May, they are on the whole coast, from Block Island to Cape Breton, and a little later are in the Bay of St. Lawrence. The early fish are generally large, and are known as seed-fish. Between the time of making their appearance, and about the middle of June, they spawn, or deposit their ova. I have made very general inquiries, from old fishermen, and especially from men all their lives engaged in fish markets, as to the probable proportion of male and female mackerel. Their judgment is quite unanimous upon about an equal division. Prof. Storer states the proportion of females as only one in ten, but I find no such authority among fishermen, who have given practical attention to these matters.

Frank T. Buckland, M. A., of London, late Surgeon to the 2d Regiment Life Guards, Editor of the "Sea and the Land," in a Lecture before the Royal Institute in 1863, which received high commendation, states, that to every pound of mackerel, there are 86,120 ova. As the average weight of seed mackerel is from one pound to one pound and a half, or more, as caught, I consider it safe and inside the authority to estimate one hundred thousand ova to every seed mackerel. As a rule, all mackerel caught previous to July first, are poor, mostly large and poor, and known commercially as No. 3, large.

The average annual returns by the Inspector General, of "No. 3, large" mackerel for the last twenty years in Massachusetts, has been fifty-four thousand six hundred and fifty barrels. By allowing two hundred and fifty fish to an inspected barrel, and taking Prof. Storer's proportion of one tenth only, as female mackerel, instead of one half, and discounting three-fourths for accidental losses to this ova, and young fish, we have as the culmination of this indiscriminate slaughter, the annual destruction of one hundred and thirty-six millions six hundred and twenty-seven thousand four hundred and eighty barrels of mackerel. This calculation is made without reference to the enormous consumptions of fresh mackerel before July, and the catch upon the coasts of Maine and all the coast of the British possessions in America, to the north-east, which must far more than treble the Massachusetts returns. Five hundred, and possibly a thousand barrels of fresh mackerel are sometimes carried into New York in a day from the fishing grounds, besides weirs and nets are set all around Cape Cod and stretch down the Eastern coast. We allow the fresh mackerel consumption a necessity, and a source of large revenue to many thousands of toilers by the sea, who are honorably engaged therein. They supply a legitimate and growing market demand, that may now be regarded a necessity. On the contrary, and in contrast, No. 3, large or spring-packed mackerel, called by the fishermen "leather belly's," rarely if ever pay the fishermen, and are of little commercial advantage, certainly none that could not be better served by the small fat stock caught in the fall, and have the merit of being good food. The early fish are eatable when fresh, with plenty of sweet butter; but when salted, become dark, thin, and tough. Salt eats up the substance, and becomes more salt. I have sold multiplied thousands of barrels, but never knew of one being eaten, always bought to ship still farther North, or West, or South. I have solicited the opinion of many leading fishermen and vessel owners, and without exception they unhesitatingly agree, that it is not profitable to catch No. 3 mackerel in the Spring to pack. It is a common remark with fishermen, that they wish there was not a mackerel caught till July.

Capt. John Banks Rich of Truro, well known throughout the fishing districts as a remarkably successful skipper for the past twenty years, has kindly furnished me with a table of his respective returns, and amount of stock, for sixteen years. These tables show conclusively, that even among the most fortunate, no money has been made in a series of years catching poor mackerel. Capt. Rich remarks, "on the whole, I think it does not pay to fit early for poor mackerel to pack." In 1864, with a crew of fourteen, Capt. Rich packed twelve hundred and seventy-five barrels caught on the hook, and stocked twenty thousand dollars. It is a peculiarity of the inspection law, that a barrel of No. 1 mackerel, valued at twenty dollars, and a barrel of No. 3 large, valued at eight dollars, have no distinctive points of difference to an uneducated eye; both are required to be not less than thirteen inches in length, and that is the only requirment; the law says, " Mackerel of the best quality not measuring less than thirteen inches, etc., shall be branded No 1." The next best quality being not less than eleven inches, etc., shall be branded No. 2. Those that remain after the above selection not less than thirteen inches, etc., shall be branded No. 3, large."

It will be observed, that the difference of twelve dollars per barrel for fish of the same size, is in *quality;* only experts can be judges of quality; and as it requires years of education to become an expert, the loop-hole in the law is big enough for an elephant. But under the present system of catching and grading, the law can scarcely be bettered. I do not intimate that a thirteen inch No. 3 mackerel is ever sold in Massachusetts for a No. 1. Our dealers are all honorable men to be sure, better than the law. It is the possibility we would guard against, and the temptation to mercenary considerations.

Fifty years ago or less, all inspectors were practical experts, mostly, men bred to the business, and all mackerel went direct from the inspector's hands to the consumers. Nearly all were packed in Massachusetts. When the Vermont farmer, or the Georgia planter bought a kit or barrel of No. 1 mackerel, he knew what he was getting — so he does now. That modern system of metamsichosis, or transmutation known as *reinspected*, had not been cradled. To-day, probably, nearly one half the mackerel sold in Boston are reinspected; and the balance are reinspected with Boston hands in nearly every State in the Union. With only the Yankee privilege of guessing, we should guess, there were a car-load of Boston hands doing service outside of Massachusetts. As no States outside of New England, have laws referring to mackerel, repacking is done as interest dictates. We are not speaking to the prejudice of any part of the country. Nobody is cheated, as we can see; competition regulates the prices.

A kit of No 1 mackerel can be bought in St. Paul, or St. Joe for one dollar and a half, when the price on Long Wharf for the genuine article is two dollars and a half. The market is demoralized, but as a rule, East or West, the purchaser gets all he pays for. But he does not get what he wants, and as he will not buy the second time what he does not want, the best trade is lost, and more and more. A million barrels of mackerel a year, with the conditions favorable, must be regarded a moderate estimate for this country, with forty millions to feed, and a large export trade to supply. Not five pounds to every individual. As our boundaries have stretched from the old Atlantic belt of thirteen states to the Pacific slope, and up and down the Western valleys, we have not added a pound to the consumption, but with homœopathic skill, reduced the allowance to a single mackerel to every man, woman, and child in the country. By way of contrast, I refer to Scotland, whose Herring Fisheries in 1855, produced in round numbers, nine hundred thousand barrels, employing seventy thousand men and eleven thousand vessels.

As we have taken so successfully to eating oat-meal, may we not take another lesson of the hardy Scotch, and learn to eat more fish? Surely if eating oat-meal and herring have given them brawn and brain, they may be proud of both. Dryden did not mean the Gaels, when he said, "Brawn without brain is theirs." In 1860, there were employed in the Irish herring fisheries, fifty-seven thousand men and boys, and over fourteen thousand vessels and boats. The Dutch and Scandinavian fisheries are enormous, the fisheries of Norway being its leading business. In 1865, a World's Convention, or Congress upon the Fisheries was held at Bergen, Norway, delegates from all parts of Europe were in attendance, and important matters touching the Fisheries were discussed.

Probably there never was a time in our history, when a cheap food-supply would be so welcome and prophetic. Commercial prostrations, and idle machinery have revived the old question of cheap living. If it has come to labor at a dollar a day, it is coming to fish as a far greater factor in settling the problem of cheap living, than all the Political Economy in the world. Physicians are agreed that a more general fish diet would tend to much more general health. It is our pleasant undertaking to show how it may be made cheap and available. Whenever Christ fed the multitudes, it was not bread and meat only, but loaves and fishes. At that last interview by the shores of Tiberius, the last miracle of which we have record, was filling the nets of the fishermen, who had toiled all night and caught nothing. "As soon as they were come to land, they saw a fire of coals there, and fish laid thereon and bread." "Jesus then cometh, and taketh bread and giveth them, and fish likewise." In the annual report of the Commissioners on Inland Fisheries for 1875, they remark in conclusion, "In the economy of living, after bread and meat comes fish, by no means the least healthy of the three. As the population increases, the necessity of procuring additional food presses, with increasing force, upon the energy and resources of the people. The successful culture of fish is no longer a matter of doubt."

The lamented Mr. Burlingame, our minister to China in 1865, who had great opportunities for observation, said, "We had yet much to learn from the so-called barbarians, and among other things, the culture of fish; in China, an acre of water is much more productive than an acre of land." Apply this rule to the million of square miles, not acres, of fishing-grounds, which we have as our right, and allow one hundred thousand fishermen, and we have a lordly domain of twenty thousand acres to every fisherman from Cape Race to Barnagat. A farm broader and longer than the famous ranches of the Pampas, to you and your assigns forever, free from all encumbrance and taxes. Europe estimated the fisheries of America beyond price. England, France, Spain and Portugal, at one time, contended for the prize, and the two first named, fought more than a hundred years for the supremacy. During the whole of the sixteenth century, colony after colony were sent to the New World to establish settlements. Millions of treasure, and tens of thousands of lives were lost, and not a foot-hold was made, till the settlements were made in the interests of the fisheries. Says the historian: "So of New England navigation and commerce, the fisheries furnished the first articles of export, and laid the foundation of the great marts of trade." Said Elbridge Gerry, when discussing a resolution upon the treaty of peace, and insisting upon the full privilege of the fisheries: "It is not fish, simply, that gentlemen sneer at, it is gold."

In 1690, when one of the ancient ministers of Portsmouth wished to reprove some of his congregation for their worldliness and depravity, and told them of the pious habits of their fathers who came to this howling wilderness to enjoy the pure principles of religion, he was interrupted by one of his congregation, replying, "Sir, you certainly mistake the matter, our ancestors did not come here on account of their religion, but to fish." A slight digression would open a field too broad for this paper. It would lead us at the siege of Louisburg, where the fishermen beat down that Dunkirk of the West, and a fisherman was Knighted for his valor; where Phipps, born a poor fisherman, led in the expedition against Canada, for which service he became Sir William Phipps, and the Governor of Massachusetts. If I am not mistaken, the only Americans that ever received that mark of honor on American soil, were these two fishermen. It would lead us to see how these services of our sailors and soldiers to the Mother Country, prepared them for the time of trial in the near future. At the siege of Louisburg were Thornton and Bradford and Gridley, who afterwards laid out the works on Bunker Hill. It would lead us to say, what history admits, that the fisheries lead to the Revolutionary War, and to the dissolution of the Crown. In the discussion of this subject we have referred to two perils which are fast wasting away the mackerel fisheries of North America.

First, The use of the purse, or deep-sea seine. Second, The catching of number three, large, or seed-fish, to salt for market. We have advocated the abandoning of the seines, and a return to the old system, by which the fish were fed, fatted, and kept near the shores and coasts; and the abandoning of the unprofitable spring fishing, whereby the propagation of mackerel is destroyed. The reasonable and practicable result of this new departure would be: 1, a rapid increase of mackerel; 2, only number one and two fat mackerel would be caught; 3, inspection laws be made much simpler and much more effective; 4, the size as a rule would regulate the quality and price; 5, the catch would be abundant for the demands of business ; 6, prices would be regulated by the laws of supply and demand with other standard commodities in the markets of the world ; 7, a million barrels of mackerel would fall short of the demand based upon the catch and prices of 1831, and 1851 ; 8, the maximum and minimum standards would be subject to light extremes ; 9, cheaper vessels and outfits would require less capital ; 10, capital would seek the business in all its branches for remunerative investment. We also advocate as a necessity a placing of Bounty upon all vessels engaged in the mackerel and codfishing business. We know it will be said that the reduction upon the duties of salt settled that question. It is evident, however, that surprising changes have taken place the last quarter of a century in our entire maritime business, and new laws have been made, and others must be made to save our commerce, or within the next decade it will be swept from the face of the ocean. The expansion of market commodities at minimum prices, is wonderfully illustrated by the statistics of our own country.

In 1818, there were inspected in Massachusetts, forty-seven thousand barrels of mackerel, which was the largest of any year in its history. It was regarded a good year for mackerel, and a great many wondered where all the mackerel went, and who ate them ? In 1820, two hundred and thirty-six thousand barrels were inspected, and all found a ready market. In 1831, the returns were three hundred and eighty-three thousand barrels, and no complaints of surplus stock. If any should think my standard of a million barrels per annum a fancy estimate, let me call your attention again to figures. At the ratio of expansion during the thirteen years from 1818 to 1831, we should need in 1890, nearly two millions of barrels. There need, than, be no doubt about the capacity of the country to consume all the mackerel that can be caught, however rapid the increase. It is almost an incalculable misfortune to narrow down a great food commodity, at a time in our economy when it should be expanded to its fullest capacity.

I may not be expected to define how a reform apparently so radical, of this magnitude, may be accomplished. I submit, however, that there is nothing staggering, or insuperable proposed; and that the promise is more than commensurate with the work to be done. Enlightened discussion must make the reform more and more apparent, and open a perfect way. But I may be expected to offer such suggestions as a careful study of the subject demands. After a little more experience and agitation, that part of the question involving seines, will, no doubt, settle itself. Intelligent and enlightened men are quick to see their interests, and are joined to no idols that promise only continued losses. A general understanding that no new purchases could be made; and a few years would witness the last of these fish destroyers. While the seines and outfits on hand last, quite probable vessels will be fitted for both seining and hooking to some extent. For suppressing the catch of poor mackerel we must look to legislation. A practical representation in the legislatures of the States on the sea-board most interested, would no doubt secure the appointing of a Committee from such States. This Committee might consider a well-devised system of co-operation to secure facts, statistics, etc., and present the same to Congress, asking for the appointing of a National Fish Board, such as England already has, and such as would have saved this country millions during the last decade. A National Fish Board would unquestionably do more to settle the vexed questions, which almost necessarily must arise from time to time by our fishermen in British waters, and reconcile all parties, than all the courts in the Provinces with an occasional sugar-plum of five millions of dollars thrown into the bargain. This Board in conference with a similar representation from the Provinces, and the English Fish Board referred to, could no doubt devise a satisfactory law. As the whole coast and shores of our neighbors to the North-East, have interests identical with our own, in the preservation of mackerel, they must come under the same law; consequently every step of the way must be mutually co-operative. My reference to legislation is no new thing under the sun, or new theory, as referring to mackerel, only one of Mr. Phillips' lost arts. More than two hundred years ago, this same question presented itself to the early fishermen of Massachusetts: the old law-makers and law-keepers. All questions with them, that could not be settled by prayer, and their trusty king's arm, must be settled by legislation. So in June, 1670, the General Court at Plymouth passed the following order:

"Whereas, we have formerly seen great inconvenience of taking mackerel at unseasonable times, whereby their increase is greatly diminished, and that it hath been proposed to the Court of the Massachusetts, that some course might be taken for preventing the same, this Court doth enact, that henceforth no mackerel shall be caught, except for spending (eating) while fresh, before the first of July annually, on penalty of the loss of the same, the one half to the colony, and the other to the informer."

On motion of William Clark, a merchant of Plymouth, in 1684, the Court enacted a law prohibiting the seining of mackerel in any part of the colony. The seines of these old colony days were the same as the common mackerel nets used by thousands all around the shores by our fishermen of to-day.

The report of a select committee of Parliament in 1833, on the British Channel fisheries, contains many interesting facts; among several suggestions, the revision of statutes, relative to the destruction of spawn and young fish, and to the use of particular kinds of nets. I am also informed by Prof. Buchland, of London, before referred to, and with whom I have lately enjoyed an interview, that the English laws are becoming more and more forcible every year, as to the kind of seines, and the time of using them. Modern legislation at home, has laid its protecting hand upon the inland and harbor fisheries, with wonderful success.

We have laws to protect the herring, the shad, the alewives, the salmon, the smelt; even the sea-spider — the lobster, has friends at Court. This is all well. The few alewives that visit the old homestead, should be encouraged in their annual pilgrimages, and their visit made pleasant; so should all others, even to a greater extent; but the whole aggregate is a fraction compared with the value and importance of the ocean fishery, under discussion.

Benj. P. Ware, Esq., of Marblehead, writing to Dr. John P. Ordway, President of the Massachusetts Fish and Game Association, of the success of the legislature for protection of smelt, speaks of the wholesale wasteful methods of slaughtering fish with seines and trawls, especially in the spawning season. Mr. Ordway adds to the Commissioners' Report, "The smelt law has exceeded the most sanguine expectations. Many persons have, to my knowledge, made from ten to twelve dollars a day collecting smelt with hook and line."

Our fishing privileges in the British-American waters alone, have lately, by a high tribunal, been placed at an enormous value, on which the annual interest at five per cent, is two hundred and fifty thousand dollars. American fishermen and merchants should be able to realize the fullest capacity from such a golden fleece. But experience, from a higher tribunal, declares such an estimate a fiction, unless timely protection is extended to the fishermen, by legislative enactment, and the restoration of Bounty by the government. Stronger arguments than those that came from Halifax, are the empty pockets of our brave fishermen, and the shrinking fortunes of enterprising merchants. It has long been the opinion of eminent statesmen and political economists, that the fisheries of the United States should be stimulated and encouraged by government bounties; not only as a protection to business so perilous and precarious, and that involves such wide-distributing interests; but especially of maintaining a large fleet of fishermen, as a nursery for our ocean marine in peace, and for our navy in war. Such aid can no more be called sectional, than a subsidy for ocean-postage, or an appropriation for deepening the mouths of the Mississippi. It would be returned two-fold to every State in the Union; directly, in cheaper goods, indirectly, in the extra consumption of cotton, hemp, pork, flour, copper, iron, lead, timber and other commodities that enter largely into building, equipping and sustaining the fisheries.

The laws of compensation and reciprocity are rarely so direct, and perhaps no other business fosters such material dependencies. The trim fishing craft that passes Sandy Hook, or Cape Cod, is the joint product of national supply and demand. The axe of the New England ship-builder echoes along our western rivers. The thousand busy hands in our shops are keeping time with other thousand hands a thousand miles away, whose united labor benefits all. If it is a legitimate function of the government to extend support to a public enterprise in time of need, the present condition of our fisheries, and their want of self-support need only be shown, to receive attention commensurate with the necessity. Comparatively a meagre amount, less, annually, than the cost of a first-class sloop-of-war, would revive the prosperity of our waning fishing communities, and build up a safe-guard for the country. A penny-wise policy is never wise, and all great nations honor a liberal construction of obligation toward their fishermen and sailors. The fishermen have always been loyal and daring. It was a Marblehead fisherman that recovered the first British flag, and hoisted the first American flag. They captured seven hundred and thirty-three merchantmen during the war of the Revolution. The old towns of Plymouth, Marblehead, Beverly, and many others, that prospered under the days of bounty-distribution, and did valiant service in the war of the Revolution, and in 1811 to 1814, will, erelong, witness the last dismantled fisherman, and the last sail upon the ocean.

In 1798, Dr. Freeman, Secretary of the New England Historical Society, wrote, that the towns of Cape Cod " were full of inhabitants." An empty jail and deserted Court Houses were appropriate commentaries upon a thriving people, whose seamen were favorably known in every port of the world. Since the withdrawal of government bounty, the number of Bankers from the District of Barnstable, embracing Cape Cod, has probably decreased three hundred per cent. Empty dwellings, grass-grown, tide-washed wharves, and abandoned warehouses are the reminders of once active and prosperous communities. The failures on the Cape have become so general, and the results so disastrous that serious alarm is prevailing, and the fearful question, "what are we going to do" is being repeated.

Local papers, full of apprehension, are encouraging the fishermen to hold out another season, hoping for "better luck" next year. A few years more like the last two or three, and the fleet of fifteen hundred to two thousand sail of New England fishermen will have sank their value, and the cities and towns, built up during the last fifty years by their hardy toil, must fall to decay, like Tyre and Sidon, which were founded by the Phœnecian fishermen, and were the commercial marts of their age.

France pays liberal bounties to her fishermen, and as a result has the largest tonnage engaged in the Bank Fishery of any section in the world. Nor do the bounties cheapen the goods at home, as the price is always well-sustained in their markets.

In 1744, the year before the fall of Louisburg, which wonderful fortress of the North had been built to protect French fisheries, so successful had their business become on the American coast, that five hundred and sixty-four ships, employing twenty-seven thousand five hundred men, were engaged, securing one million four hundred and forty-one thousand five hundred quintals of fish. The advantage of this position, and the success of their fisheries had long been an itching palm to the colonists. And as showing the value of this gigantic stronghold, the very next year, 1745, less than one hundred ships came to America from France. A hundred years later, under neutral relations, the French fleet reached four hundred and fourteen ships, barks, and brigs.

When in 1778, France nobly volunteered a helping hand amid our perilous fortunes of war, her fishermen on the banks were recalled to man her ships of war. But the conditions of that assistance were especially and carefully guarded touching her relations to the Fisheries, so that in no event France should loose a jot of her rights, etc. It was even stipulated, that " in certain contingencies, the fisheries should be used equally between them, and the securing of them jointly, to the total exclusion of Great Britian." Previous to this time, England had opposed any concessions to France, saying, " Her Fisheries were worth more than all Canada." These peeps at history in the great drama that brought Peace and Independence to the colonies, are not insignificant. Mr. Senac says : " The Codfishery is a productive industry, and it furnishes more than a fifth out of our whole number of seamen, and by far the best portion of them. There is no cheaper, better, or more useful school for the formation of seamen for the navy, and none is more capable of extension and development."

July 22, 1857, the National Assembly of France declared a bounty without detail on codfish, from January 1852 to July 1861, as follows:

Fifty francs per man of the crew employed and possessing a drying place.
Thirty francs per man of the crew employed without a drying place.
Twenty francs per Metric quintal (220½ lbs) of dry codfish.
Sixteen francs per Metric quintal of dry codfish.
Twelve francs per Metric quintal of dry codfish.
  Subject to sundry relations and conditions.

In the Franco-Prussian war the great French fleet of fishermen on the banks were called home to man her ships and assist in the national protection. According to the annual statistical report of France, the Newfoundland and Bank Codfisheries of 1875 were thirty-one and a half millions kilogrammes (2 lbs. 3¼ ozs.) valued at fifteen millions of francs. Thus, by a judicious administration of moderate bounty, a valuable national industry is sustained, and at the same time, an invaluable national school is maintained for the navy and marine. It must be admitted that no nation better nurses and protects her own resources, and is less dependent upon her neighbors than France.

A STATE PAPER OF THE KINGDOM OF THE NETHERLANDS.

"An Act of 6th of March, 1818, for the encouragement of the Island Codfishery. Art. I. There shall be paid out of the public Treasury a premium of five hundred gilders (two hundred dollars) for every voyage of each vessel, which, for account of our subjects, is fitted out in this kingdom, and shall sail from one of its ports during the years 1818, 1819 and 1820."

In the year ending 1835, when Parliament granted £143,790 to stimulate the Scotch Fisheries, and to poor Ireland only £12,000, it is a notable fact that Scotch fish, valued at over £60,000 were annually exported to Ireland, notwithstanding the advantages, naturally, of the Irish Fisheries. The Bounty systems of

England and other nations might be still further perused, showing that the United States stands nearly alone in her policy of withholding direct encouragement to her Ocean Fisheries.

I have penned these pages, feeling that this subject has not received desired attention, and with the earnest hope, that hereby other minds, always ready for every good word and work, may exercise their influence in its behalf. The direct interests presented you this evening, have not been learned from books, or received second-hand, but are the results of a life-long and familiar experience with the people and their business. I misunderstand our home feeling, and the honest sentiment of the great West and South, where I have had considerable business experience, and extensive opportunity for observation and comparison, if the sympathy of the land is not with the fishermen of New England. At the best, the fisherman secures a hard-earned pittance. If a few, by hardy toil, sacrifice, and strict frugality, have arrived at competence and comfort, the many have forfeited life in the struggle, or come to manhood with no provision for old age.

While the productive centre of our country is the great River Valley and its tributaries, and the Western Slope of the Continent, the Eastern Coast, as nearest to the millions of Europe, must always remain its substantial base. As our great cities and towns are brought nearer and nearer to each other by the rapid appliances of transit, so much the more our unity consists in our increasing diversity of interests, and our kinship in national identity.

Printed by Libri Plureos GmbH in Hamburg, Germany